THE BIG CATCH OF FISH

A READ ALOUD BIBLE STORY BOOK FOR KIDS – THE NEW TESTAMENT STORY OF JESUS, FROM THE SHORES OF GALILEE TO THE CROSS AND RESURRECTION. THE EASTER STORY, RETOLD FOR BEGINNERS

JENNIFER CARTER

Illustrated by
HATTIE MILLIDGE

Copyright © 2019 by Jennifer Carter

All rights reserved.

No part of this book may be reproduced in any form or by any electronic or mechanical means, including information storage and retrieval systems, without written permission from the author, except for the use of brief quotations in a book review.

Cover Illustration by Hattie Millidge of Harri Tea Designs

Edited by Daphne Parsekian

Scripture quotations from The World English Bible (WEB) is a Public Domain (no copyright) Modern English translation of the Holy Bible.

Scriptures taken from the Holy Bible, New International Version®, NIV®. Copyright © 1973, 1978, 1984, 2011 by Biblica, Inc.™ Used by permission of Zondervan. All rights reserved worldwide. www.zondervan.com The "NIV" and "New International Version" are trademarks registered in the United States Patent and Trademark Office by Biblica, Inc.™

Scripture quotations marked (NLT) are taken from the Holy Bible, New Living Translation, copyright © 1996, 2004, 2015 by Tyndale House Foundation. Used by permission of Tyndale House Publishers, Inc., Carol Stream, Illinois 60188. All rights reserved.

1

INTRODUCTION FOR PARENTS

The Big Catch of Fish is a re-imagining of the Easter story and is based on some stories that you'll find in a book called the Bible.

It tells the story of Jake, a boy living by and fishing on the lakeside in Galilee, as he gets to know Jesus and his friends.

These stories really happened, but the details in this story are imagined. But who's to say that this isn't exactly just what happened?

Jesus is spoken of as a friend in this book, so we haven't capitalised any words that relate to Him, as you might in a book for grown-ups.

If you're a grown-up, you likely know what happens in the Easter story, and you also know how it ends. You may want to listen to Chapters 11-13, before deciding whether it's suitable for your child to listen to.

JENNIFER CARTER

Enjoy taking your child on a journey in their imagination with this story!

2

THE BIG CATCH OF FISH

My dad is the best dad in the world. Some of the best times in my life are when Dad takes me out on the boat. We go out fishing and catch dozens of fish. I love the way they wriggle and shimmer silver in the moonlight, and I love to watch as Dad's strong arms pull in the nets full of fish.

After hours on the water together, we glide back across the calm waters of the lake through the soft mist of the morning. As everyone else is waking up and starting their day, it's time to sell our catch of fish, right from the edge of the boat, before taking a well-earned break.

I was only six when my mother died. After that, it was just me and my dad. I don't remember much about Mother. Sometimes Dad talks about her. When he tells me stories, I can almost imagine what she was really like.

Now it's just me and my dad. It's been that way for a long time, and to be honest, I quite like it that way.

Of course, I had no idea that my life was perfect. That is, until one day it wasn't.

It started when my dad got sick—I mean really sick. He was so sick that he was sent away by the men who lead our village. When he left, I was left on my own, with no family around me. I was just a boy on his own trying not to give up hope. For a long time, my belly ached, not from hunger (although I was often hungry) but from missing him.

I missed his big smile, the way he wrapped me up in his hug, and his laughter. Boy, we used to laugh so much together. I missed the old times, and I yearned for just one more fishing trip out on the lake.

Without Dad to talk to and laugh with, the days drag on, and time passes slowly. Now it's just me on my own.

Well, I guess I'm not completely alone. Sometimes I play with my best friend Jaala down by the lake. We love to pick up stones and see which of us can throw them out into the water the farthest. She can run faster than I can, but I can usually throw the stone farther than she can.

The fishermen who live and work here by the lakeside are kind to me, especially Peter and Andrew. They're good friends and look out for me. Sometimes they ask me to help out, inviting me to sit and help them while they clean and wash the nets. In return, they share their catch with me, and we cook and eat the freshly caught fish together over an open fire on the beach.

THE BIG CATCH OF FISH

The day I want to tell you about starts just like any other day.

"Come on, Jake," calls Peter. "Hurry up!"

The fishermen have been up all night and haven't caught a thing. No fish means no money. No wonder Peter sounds unhappy.

"Be right there!" I say, bleary eyed.

It's a bad day for everyone when there's no fish. Tonight we'll be hungry ... again.

We've had a bad run of things for the last week or two, and everyone's getting worried. If we can't catch fish, how will we eat?

The sun is rising over the hills now, and we sit on the empty shore, scrubbing and cleaning the nets. Everyone's talking about why we've had such a poor catch.

"It was too calm," says one.

"Too cool. A bit of sun today will bring out the fish," says another.

"If only we'd gone out a bit farther, we'd have struck lucky," says Andrew.

As we're talking, the shoreline starts to fill with people.

"It's Jesus!" shouts out Peter, jumping up and running over to him.

Jesus ... I've heard that name before.

At the synagogue, they've been saying bad things about him. But around the fire or out in his boat, Peter's told us some amazing stories about Jesus. I love listening to his stories and want so much for what Peter says to be true.

As I look up, I see crowds of people coming towards us from every direction. Jesus is sitting on the shore, talking to the gathering crowds.

Just then, Jesus walks over and climbs right into Peter's boat. He doesn't ask, he just strolls over and jumps in!

"Put out a little from the shore," he says.

Looking a little surprised, Peter does exactly what Jesus says.

And just like that, Jesus stands and speaks to the crowds from our boat, a short distance out from the shore.

I listen to his words, letting them wash over me like the waves on the shore. The sound of his words is interrupted by my stomach making funny rumbling noises. The sun is beating down, and it's so warm.

All I want to do right now is lie in the shade of a tree or go swimming in the lake, but Jesus tells stories that I love listening to. He's even better at storytelling than Peter. I could listen to Jesus all day.

As the sun begins to set, everyone starts for home, chatting excitedly about the things they'd heard Jesus talking about.

As the beach clears, Jesus turns and looks straight at Peter. "Put your boat out into the deep water, and let down your nets for a catch."

Peter looks up at him. "Master, we've worked all night and caught nothing. But because you say so, I'll let down the nets."

They push out from the shore, leaving me on the beach. I look out towards the boat, wondering what will happen.

After a few minutes on the lake, they are pulling in the nets.

Peter calls to the shore, "Send a second boat. There are so many fish!"

Their boat is sitting so low in the water that it is almost sinking. They must have caught hundreds of fish. It looks as if it's a record catch!

As the second boat pushes off from the shore, I run and jump in to it. I have to see for myself what is happening.

Within minutes, our nets are filled with more fish than I've ever seen. We are pulling in hundreds of fish, and it's almost as if they're jumping right into our nets. Soon the bottom of the boat is full of wet and shiny fish glittering and tickling my feet, then we're headed back to shore with our enormous catch of fish.

No-one can believe it. We've caught more than enough to fill our bellies for tonight and tomorrow, with plenty more to share.

These fishermen fish every day. They'd tried every fishing trick in the book and caught nothing last night. It seemed impossible, but Jesus has made it possible. Our nets are full to bursting with glistening silver fish!

I've never seen anything like this before—nobody has.

Everyone's laughing. Amazed. So happy.

We share the catch between us.

There's plenty for everyone.

I can barely carry all the fish I'm given, and I know at once what I must do.

I'll take some to Dad. I can't wait to tell him all about our amazing day.

3

DAD'S STORY

It's time I told you a bit more about what happened to my dad and why everything changed.

My dad was a fisherman. His dad, my grandad, was a fisherman too. I'm from a long line of fishermen. Fishing is what we do.

There's nothing we love to do more than hang out together by the lake. It's great fun to sit cleaning the nets at the lakeside, telling tall tales of the fish we've caught or the ones that got away.

I love helping push the boat out onto the waters to throw out the nets then pulling them in filled with fish.

There's nothing quite as amazing as the joy you get when you're out catching fish. Well, apart from the taste of freshly caught fish for breakfast, that is!

My life was perfect.

But then Dad got sick.

At first, it was just his skin. Something seemed to be eating his skin away. Then his fingers, his strong hands, became curled, misshapen, useless. Poor Dad ... his fishing days were over.

No more pulling in the nets for him. No more sitting around the fire telling stories and fixing the fishing nets.

As if that wasn't bad enough, they sent him away from the village, away from our home...away from me.

Nobody talks about Dad now. They don't mention him at all. I don't know why. It's like he did something wrong, but he didn't. He just got sick.

I miss him so much.

I loved it so much when he teased me, chased me, and tickled me, but I liked it best when he hugged me. He had a real bear hug, a hug where I felt completely wrapped up in it, warm and safe. When Dad held me like that, it felt like none of the bad stuff mattered anymore and that everything would be okay.

After Dad was sent away, it was hard for me. I struggled to get enough food to eat for me, let alone enough to take to Dad

Dad looks different somehow. He seems sadder. His eyes have lost their twinkle. He walks with his shoulders slumped, and his once-strong arms hang limply at his sides.

It's always good to see him, but I can't touch him. We're not allowed to hug.

Of course, I'm happy to see him, but everything is so different.

THE BIG CATCH OF FISH

I miss the old dad, the one with eyes that sparkled with laughter and who gave huge bear hugs that left me feeling breathless. It's hard to explain. I love seeing him, but inside, I feel really sad at the same time.

I visit as often as I can to take him some of the food that the fishermen have given me.

That's why I am so excited about this huge catch of fish.

Carrying as many fish as I can, I run and skip along the dusty road to see Dad.

In the distance, I see his silhouette. "Dad!" I cry out excitedly.

He smiles—a weary smile, the "I'm sorry I can't help you" smile he wears now. "It's good to see you, Jake," he says quietly.

I start telling him all about my amazing day. "Dad, you'll never believe what happened today! All night we fished but caught nothing. Then we caught more fish than you've ever seen."

He looks up, I just keep talking.

"It's Jesus. Everyone's talking about him. He came and spoke to the crowds today. There were so many people wanting to listen that he had to go out in Peter's boat! When he finished talking and everybody left, it was just us fishermen left.

It was so funny. Jesus is a carpenter, but he told Peter, who's been a fisherman all his life, to go and throw the nets out again.

I couldn't believe it when Peter listened to Jesus and did what he asked. He pushed the boat out from the shore, and soon there were so many fish that we filled not one but two boats with them and nearly sunk them both. It was amazing. If only you could've seen it!"

Dad was looking at the floor, but I knew he'd been listening. "Thanks for the fish, son. It's so good to see you looking happy."

"Everyone's talking about him, Dad. Jesus's words sound true. When he touches people, their sickness goes away."

"Son, you are forgetting one thing. No-one's allowed to touch me," he interrupts.

"You know that! They're not allowed near me. Not even Jesus could fix what's wrong with me. I'm stuck like this forever, and there's nothing this Jesus can do about it."

"But Peter said that Jesus helped his mother-in-law get better," I say, determined to tell him what I'd seen.

"Really? Peter said that?" he asks. At last he is looking me in the eye.

"Yes, Dad. Will you come and see Jesus? Just try and see, please, Dad." My voice trails off. I hardly dare to hope.

Dad looks intently at me for a few moments. "Okay, but I'm telling you, it's probably just a waste of time. Nothing will come of it. I'll get in trouble and he'll turn his back on me, just like everyone seems to have done."

"Dad, just come. We have to try," I plead.

"Okay, come back tomorrow, and we'll see if we can find Jesus and let's see if Pete is right about him."

With that, I run off with a skip in my step.

Wow, what a day! For the first time in weeks, my belly is filled to bursting. Better than that, I've had a great time with my Dad.

And it isn't just me who is feeling happier. For the first time in ages, Dad had looked at me a bit like he used to.

I might have imagined it, but I think I saw a small smile forming at the edges of his mouth, and there seemed to be a tiny twinkle in his eyes again.

Maybe, I wonder, *just maybe, things can change for the better.*

4

DAD COMES HOME

The next morning, I wake up early. I race back to see Dad, afraid that he might have changed his mind overnight.

When I arrive, I can't believe it. He is ready and waiting for me. Together, we set off on the road towards the lake, Dad limping along as best as he can.

I chatter happily about some of the stories that Peter has told me about Jesus. It's just so good to be spending time with my dad again.

Peter had told me that Jesus is staying with some friends in Capernaum in a house just by the edge of the lake.

Because of his sickness, Dad isn't allowed to go into the village, so we just find a shady spot under an olive tree just outside the village. From our vantage point, we'll be able to see everyone setting out towards the village of Magdala. All we can do is to sit and wait, hoping to catch a glimpse of Jesus.

We wait a long time. As it grows hotter, the number of flies buzzing around our feet and heads seems to grow.

Just as we are about to give up and go home, we see Jesus. He's walking away from us, on the path leaving the village. This is our chance!

"There he is! Quick, Dad. Let's go!"

Dad gets to his feet, moving as fast as he can. I can see it's a huge effort for him as his face grimaces with pain at each step, but he keeps going. Soon he's walking so fast I can barely keep up with him.

As we catch up with him, Jesus must hear our footsteps behind him because he turns around. I thought he'd look surprised, but he seems to be totally calm.

I can hardly believe what happens next. My dad throws himself onto the ground in front of Jesus.

I have no idea what to expect. What will happen now?

As Dad looks up at Jesus, a single tear rolls down his dust-covered face. "Jesus, if you want to, you can heal me. Make me clean again," he whispers, his voice hoarse and quiet from his sickness.

Then the impossible happens.

Jesus reaches out and touches Dad.

Touches him! Jesus touches the one it's forbidden for anyone to touch, but he reaches out and touches my dad, the leper.

Jesus speaks softly, "I want to. Be made clean," all the while not taking his eyes away from my dad's eyes.

As I look on, I can't believe what I am seeing. I watch as Dad's broken skin becomes new. His oddly shaped fingers twist and mould themselves back to normal. The withered muscles on his arms twitch and grow big and strong again. His misshapen feet rearrange themselves and become straight and whole again. And it all happens right in front of my eyes.

I can't believe what I am seeing.

My dad, the leper, is completely changed right in front of me. Instead of the sick, sad dad, my happy, fun dad is back. He's my dad again, just like I remember him before he got sick.

And it is all because of Jesus.

Once he realises what's happening, Dad starts to move, trying out his body. A smile lights up his face as he discovers he can move freely again and that the pain is gone from his body.

Dad breaks into a dance, flinging his arms and legs wildly in all directions. We watch Dad dancing this crazy, happy dance.

Suddenly, we are all laughing. Dad's laughing, I'm laughing, and Jesus's friends are laughing. And then a huge smile breaks out on Jesus's face, and he's laughing too!

When finally the laughter stops, Dad looks at Jesus. Slowly, he kneels on the dusty road and bows his head before Jesus.

It feels like we are in the temple again. There is something holy and special about this moment.

"Go to the priest. Let him see and confirm that you're clean," says Jesus.

Clean? He's clean! He really is clean again!

I can't tell you what this means. I've felt so ashamed having a dad who was unclean, a leper. You can't imagine how it's hurt me to hear the neighbours call him 'unclean'. But in one moment, everything has changed.

He's clean again. He's strong and well and happy! My mind is buzzing with what this all means.

At last, Dad can come home, like I've dreamt he would. We can go fishing together like we used to.

Everything that was wrong is right again.

Thank you, Jesus.

I blink my eyes, wondering if somehow it's all a dream. Can it possibly be true?

And then it happens, the moment I've longed and waited for.

Dad looks at me and opens his arms wide, and I know exactly what to do. I run into them, and his strong arms wrap themselves around me in a bear hug.

Oh, how I've missed Dad's bear hug! Wrapped in Dad's arms, it feels as if everything will be okay now. I'm home and safe, and all the wrong things have somehow been made right.

5

JESUS MEETS MY BEST FRIEND

Life's great again. Dad is out in the boats, fishing again. Everything's back to normal, just like it was before he got sick. I guess you could say that it's even better than before because now I know just how good my life really is!

A few weeks have passed since that day when Jesus touched my dad. We've told everyone the story about what Jesus did, and we've heard some amazing stories about Jesus from others.

Today, the sun is shining down on the lake, and I can see the hills beyond reflected in the still waters. It's a perfect day to go fishing.

"Dad, can I help you with the fish today?"

"No, son. Why don't you go and have some fun? It's time for your dad to catch our supper for a change. You've worked hard enough these past few months."

With a few hours free, my thoughts turn to my friend, Jaala. I'll go and play with Jaala!

We love to play down at the lake together, playing games, throwing stones, and running races. Whatever we play, we have such fun together, and I can hardly wait to see the smile when I knock at her door.

When I arrive at the village, the streets are thronging with people —people who've come to see Jesus.

I dodge through the back streets, eager to get to Jaala's house. When I arrive, there's no sign of Jaala. It's all quiet. It feels as if something's wrong.

That's when I hear it...the sound of people crying.

Jaala's dad opens the door. He's a leader at our local synagogue, which makes him pretty important in our village.

It's strange for him to be at home at this time of the day, and this is the first time I realise that something might be wrong.

"Where's Jaala?" I ask him.

His eyes don't look up from the floor. "She's sick. She's really sick. My beautiful girl... I don't know what to do!"

I run through the door to see my friend. She is lying on the bed, still and pale, unmoving. Her mother is sitting beside her, tears running down her face.

I know at once that this is serious. We all know that life is fragile. Every family has lost someone they love.

THE BIG CATCH OF FISH

Then I remember Dad's story and Jesus. If anyone can help, he can.

Turning to her dad, I urge him, "Jesus! You have to take her to Jesus!"

Then I'm telling her dad the stories of everything I've seen Jesus do. I'm telling him about the amazing catch of fish and the touch of his hand that healed Dad.

Jesus has changed everything for me, maybe he can for Jaala too.

"Perhaps this Jesus is sent from God. Where can I find him?" asks Jaala's dad.

At that moment, we hear a commotion outside—noise, people, and shouting.

Jesus has returned from the other side of the lake in Peter's boat. Everyone's calling out to him, and the crowds are pushing in around him.

But Jaala's dad doesn't waste a minute. He strides out quickly, and I follow, struggling to keep up with him.

We push our way through the swarms of people, knowing that every minute counts…that life is fragile…that even now Jaala is struggling for breath. All I can think about is her lying pale on her bed, breathing so quietly.

The crowds part for Jaala's dad, respectful of his position as leader of the synagogue.

It's not long and we're standing in front of Jesus. Jaala's dad falls to his knees before Jesus.

This feels awkward. I mean, he's pretty much the most important guy in our town, and here he is, on his knees, begging Jesus to help him.

"It's my daughter, my little girl... If you'll just place your hand on her, she'll live," he pleads.

I keep looking at Jesus, wondering what will happen next.

With a look, the slightest nod of his head, he gestures to Jaala's dad to lead the way. "Don't be afraid. Just believe," he says. So few words, yet such power in each word.

Jaala's dad pushes his way through the crush of people. Jesus follows close behind, his friends following him close on his heels.

The crowds are suffocating, but I keep following, eager to see what Jesus will do.

Suddenly, Jesus stops and stands still. "Who touched me?"

Who touched him? What is he thinking? Everyone's crowded around, pushed up against each other. How can he ask who touched him?

Even his friend Peter is wondering what he can mean. "Master, everyone's pressing in and jostling you. How can you ask who touched you?" says Peter.

Jesus replies, "Someone did touch me. I felt power go out from me."

At this, a woman turns to him, trembling and weeping, and falls down before him.

Jesus looks down into her tear-stained face. "Daughter, you can smile again. Your faith has made you well. Go and live your life in peace."

At his words, the woman breaks into a smile. She looks as if she has just been given an amazing gift.

And I know something amazing has just happened. Even though I don't understand it, Jesus has done it again.

There has to be hope for Jaala too!

But, just as Jesus is speaking to her, a servant comes from Jaala's house. "Don't trouble the teacher," he whispers to Jaala's dad. "Your daughter is dead."

Jaala's dad puts his face in his hands to hide his grief. For a few moments, he'd hoped for the impossible, but this awful news shatters his hope.

I can't believe what I'm hearing. My friend is gone, so quickly? The pain feels as if something sharp has stabbed my heart. I can't believe that we've arrived just a few minutes too late.

Every eye is on Jesus.

"Don't be afraid," says Jesus to Jaala's dad. "Only believe."

We keep walking, the crowds parting for Jesus.

As we approach Jaala's home, the sound of weeping and wailing grows louder. It's the sound of mourning. My friend Jaala—a girl, a daughter, a friend—once so full of life but now lying still and silent.

Jaala's father is weeping openly now. Huge tears are rolling down his face. His face is crumpled with sadness, and deep sobs break from his chest.

Jesus enters the house, takes one look at the girl lying pale and cold on the bed, and says, "Don't cry. She's not dead. She's just asleep."

The women's crying turns to jeers and laughter.

"Is he mad?" one woman asks.

"Anyone can see she's dead," says another.

Jesus looks into their eyes. "Why do you make such noise? The child is not dead, she's only sleeping."

Jesus leads his friends into the house, with Jaala's parents following behind, and closes the door behind them. No-one else is allowed in, not even me, her best friend.

With the door closed, I can't see anything. So I sit down on the hard ground, finding shelter from the sun in the shade of a tree, and wait.

I fix my eyes on the door of the house. I wait and wonder. What will happen? Surely it's too late. What can Jesus do now?

I don't have to wait very long. After a few minutes, Jaala appears, standing in the doorway.

She's eating something. And smiling—a great big beam of a smile.

I blink my eyes in the sunlight. I can't believe what I'm seeing. She's back! My friend is back! She's okay. It's all going to be okay.

I run and hug Jaala, so happy to have my friend back. I'm already thinking of all the fun we can have together.

I can't believe that she's well again. She was so sick, so still, but now she is full of life.

As Jesus leaves the house, I run up to him. "Thank you, Jesus, thank you!"

His smiling, warm eyes look down at me, and his face breaks into a wide smile too. Now everyone is smiling and laughing.

Jesus lifts me up and twirls me around. As we spin together, I can feel the wind in my hair and my feet swinging out crazily.

There's a wild joy about this moment as our joy and laughter chases away the tears and sadness.

6

FIVE LOAVES, TWO FISH

I can hardly believe everything that's happened since I met Jesus.

When we were tired and hungry, he helped us catch hundreds of fish.

When Dad was sick, he touched him, and now he's well.

When Jaala was lying still and dead, he touched her, and she was alive again.

He just keeps doing impossible things.

When I hear that Jesus will be up on a hillside, telling more of his stories. I just know I have to go, and I don't think that Dad will mind.

"Dad, can I go and listen to Jesus? Everyone's going up to the hillside. Please, Dad…"

"Go on then," replies Dad. "I reckon I can manage without your help today. Don't forget to take something to eat though!"

"I won't," I call as I fly out of the door, grabbing a few small loaves and a couple of fish that we'd caught fresh and cooked earlier this morning.

Joining the crowds, I follow them up to the hillside, where Jesus is already talking. We're far away from the villages along the shore. From here, on the hillside, I can see right across the lake to the hills and mountains beyond.

I find a quiet spot amidst the crowds and sit down on the grass, looking at and listening to Jesus. I'm so happy to spend time with Jesus again.

I love the sound of his words as Jesus talks; they sound true. I love the way he tells stories. When he talks about life, it's in a way that makes me feel happy, as if everything's going to be okay.

Even when the sun is at its highest, at the hottest part of the day, Jesus is still talking. There are people of all ages sitting and listening to him. Nobody's bored.

When he stops talking, he doesn't get a break. That's when queues of people come up to him, wanting him to touch them or someone they've brought to see him. Jesus speaks with them, and sometimes he touches them. I can see the joy as they smile and laugh when he makes them well again.

Time goes quickly, and I notice the sun is low in the sky. It's nearly evening. My tummy growls, and I remember that I brought some food with me and haven't eaten any yet.

THE BIG CATCH OF FISH

As I'm about to take my first bite of cooked fish, Jesus stops talking. His disciples seem to be asking a question.

I move closer to hear what they're saying.

"It's late, and we're in the middle of nowhere," says Peter. "Send these crowds away. They need to go to the villages to buy food."

Jesus turns to them. "They don't need to leave. You can give them something to eat."

Then I think about Jesus. We've been sitting here, but he's been talking all day in the hot sun. He must be hungry.

I look at my little lunch and think, *I could always eat later. Perhaps I could give my lunch to Jesus.*

Winding my way through the crowd, I push forward and approach one of Jesus's friends. I've seen him down by the lakeside before. It's Peter's brother, Andrew.

"Here's my lunch. It isn't much, but I want Jesus to have it," I whisper to him as I show him my basket of loaves and fishes.

Andrew doesn't seem too happy and turns to Jesus, saying, "Jesus, there's a boy here with five barley loaves and two fish, but what use is that to so many?"

Jesus replies, "Bring them here to me."

Smiling now, I give my little lunch to Andrew, hoping that Jesus will enjoy eating it after his tiring day.

Then I watch as, my lunch in his hands, he holds it up to the sky. He blesses it then hands it to his friends.

His friends start wandering amongst the seated crowds, handing out my lunch.

Hang on, Jesus. That's meant for you! I think, disappointed that Jesus won't get to have any of my lunch after all.

I wonder what will happen when the food runs out. Yet the disciples keep walking through the crowds. They keep handing out the bread and fish.

It doesn't take long before a happy murmur runs through the crowd. That's the sound of full tummies filled with my little lunch of fish and bread.

There must be hundreds of people here. Now everyone's eating, chatting, and happily talking about all they've heard today. And all they've had to eat is just a few loaves and fishes.

All these people have just eaten my simple lunch. How is that even possible?

Even Jesus's friends are shaking their heads. We're all wondering about what's just happened before our eyes.

And then it dawns on us. He's just done the impossible! Again!

Finally, everyone in the crowd has had enough to eat. It's only then that I see Jesus take some food from the baskets. He looks up to the sky and gives thanks again before eating his own lunch. I'm so happy Jesus did get to share my lunch after all!

Jesus seems to know exactly what I'm thinking because he looks right at me. Slowly, a big smile spreads across his face, and he reaches into the basket, holds out some bread, and offers it to me.

As I take it from his hand, he smiles.

My little lunch has fed the crowds and Jesus, with enough left over for me to have some too!

I think he's happy to have fed the hungry crowds who've sat listening here all day. And I think he's happy that I shared my lunch.

I'm left puzzling just how it is that Jesus made the impossible possible—again.

7

JESUS, JAALA AND ME

I've been spending time with Dad, helping him when he's fishing, cleaning the nets, and just spending time with him. Dad's so happy that he's given me the day off again. No work today for me!

I'm so happy that Dad's well enough to go fishing again. As for me, I'm loving spending time playing with my friends, just being a kid again.

Today, I can't wait to see Jaala. I find her helping her mother in the kitchen.

"Please, can Jaala and I go outside?" I ask Jaala's mother.

"Go on then, you two," says her mum as we run out into the sunshine.

Racing along the edge of the lake, I think about how things used to be, when Dad had to go away and Jaala was so sick. But because of Jesus, everything's okay again.

We run up the little track away from our village and into the fields beyond. It's so good to be outside, having fun, running around, and feeling the wind on my face.

After a while, we decide to look for somewhere cool to rest. Running around on a hot day is hard work, and the idea of resting in the shade sounds great.

We walk over to a shady olive grove. As we get closer, we're surprised to see Jesus sitting there, talking with his friends. There are no crowds this time. It's just Jesus and a few friends.

I take one look at Jaala and know what I must do. I'm going to stroll right up to Jesus and tell him.

"I have to say thank you...tell him how he's changed everything."

"But..." says Jaala, hiding behind a tree. She's not so sure it's a good idea to bother Jesus.

"Don't worry. Everything will be okay," I whisper, and before she can change her mind, I walk right over to where Jesus is sitting.

Before I can get to him, his friends stand up, blocking my way and telling me to go away. "Jesus needs to rest. Don't bother him now," says one gruffly.

I try to see past them, to see Jesus, but they block my way.

Jaala looks over at me as if to say, "I told you so."

I turn slowly, feeling stupid and embarrassed, tears coming to my eyes. I look down at the ground, wishing the tears away and hoping that Jaala doesn't notice. How foolish of me to think that Jesus would remember, to think that he'd welcome me.

THE BIG CATCH OF FISH

Then I hear his voice booming out, "Let them come!"

I turn around as his friends stand aside. All I can see now is Jesus, his face smiling, his arms open wide.

"The boy with the fish!" he chuckles as he lifts me into his arms.

He remembered. All those crowds of people and Jesus remembered me.

"Jaala, my little doe!" Smiling, he picks up Jaala and wraps her in his arms. Soon they're both laughing together, and his soft, low laugh feels like bubbles flowing along a stream.

When we finally stop laughing, I tell Jesus more of my story. I tell him how I watched as he helped Peter with the big catch of fish. How I told Dad and how Jesus touched him and made him well. How I'm not hungry every day any more.

How Dad's smiling. That he's back fishing on the lake again. How I'd told Jaala's dad to ask Jesus for help when she was sick and how happy I felt when I saw Jaala come to her front door with Jesus.

Jesus listens to everything I need to tell him.

After listening to my story, he smiles. Then he turns to his friends. "It's little ones like this who make up God's Kingdom. You must come simply, like this child, to come to God."

Then Jesus begins to talk to us about God the Father. We all sit listening for a while. It is wonderful. Just Jesus and his friends sitting in an olive grove, laughing, joking, and telling stories.

As the sun sinks lower in the sky, the time to go home comes far too soon.

As we turn to go, waving and calling out, "Goodbye," to each other, we wave until Jesus is just a dot on the horizon. How amazing to sit with Jesus as his friends.

I can hardly wait to see him again to see what might happen next.

8

MY FIRST PASSOVER

I can hardly believe it. Dad's been telling me the Passover story every year since I can remember. This year he's actually taking me to Jerusalem with him.

This is the first time I've been allowed to go with him. It's going to be my first Passover in the holy city of Jerusalem!

Leaving our nets behind, we pack a few belongings and get ready for the journey. It's going to be a long walk, taking several days. What an adventure!

As we set out on the road, I beg Dad to tell me the Passover story again.

"Our people, the Israelites, became slaves in Egypt. For hundreds of years, our families lived and died as slaves."

"God had called us His people, the ones He loves and calls His own. He promised our forefathers that one day we would return to our homeland, but for many years, it seemed as if He had broken His promise."

"We were slaves, living in a strange land. After four hundred years of silence, many people thought He'd forgotten us."

"So what happened, Dad?" I asked.

"He sent someone to free us—a man, a prince. His name was Moses. Moses was not afraid of their ruler, Pharaoh."

"He told him to let God's people go. But Pharaoh refused, so God sent terrible plagues to Egypt. He sent jumping frogs and biting insects. He sent swarms of flies and waves of locusts. He turned the rivers of Egypt into blood."

"Then He sent a terrible storm. There was thunder, lightning, and hailstones, followed by darkness for three days. Even then, Pharaoh wouldn't let God's people go. He was too stubborn to change his mind."

"Finally, there came the night that changed everything. God sent the worst plague of all: The angel of death visited every firstborn child and animal. That night, there was death in every Egyptian home."

"So if I'd lived Egypt, as your firstborn son, I would have died too?"

"Only if you were an Egyptian. God warned His people, the Israelites. He told them to make a sacrifice, to find and kill a pure lamb and paint its blood on the doorposts. This would be a special sign, and He promised that the angel of death would pass over any home with the blood on their doorposts. And that's exactly what happened."

"Death came to every home in Egypt. From the firstborn child to the firstborn animal, from Pharaoh's palace to the lowliest prisoner in the dungeon, many died that night. But God's people, who had trusted in God to save them, were kept safe. Every home where they'd painted blood on the doorposts, God's angel of death passed over them."

"Is that why it's called the Passover?"

"Yes, that's right, because the angel of death passed over our homes that night. It was on that day Pharaoh agreed to let us go. We packed up our homes and belongings and left the land of Egypt. We were a free people once again."

"That's a great story, Dad. Have you got any more stories like that one?"

Dad has plenty of stories to tell. It's a long walk to Jerusalem, but his stories help me forget my tired feet and the long journey.

The closer we get to Jerusalem, the bigger the crowds on the road seem to get. It seems that everyone's going up to celebrate Passover in the Holy City.

"We're nearly there. Look, that's Jericho in the distance. Not long now..." says Dad. "We'll find something to eat there and take a rest."

9

AT THE GATES OF JERICHO

As we get closer to Jericho, the road gets busy. I hold on to Dad's hand tightly, worried I might lose sight of him in the crowds.

Then I see a familiar face ahead on the road. "It's Jesus!" I shout happily.

Dragging Dad behind me, I push my way forward through the crowds.

Can all this really be happening? My friend Jesus is here, on the road to Jericho. It's so good to see his familiar face.

We become part of the crowd, all of us following Jesus and his friends along the road. I can't help thinking that Jesus must feel tired after the long walk from Galilee. He must need a rest rather than the crowds pushing around him.

As we approach the gates of the city, I hear one voice shouting loudly, above the noise of the crowd, "Jesus, son of David, have mercy."

Some of those following Jesus turn to the man, telling him to be quiet.

We're so close to the city now, I can't wait to find somewhere to sit down and rest. As I'm dreaming of a cool spot and a long drink, I hear the voice cry out again, "Jesus, have mercy on me."

I watch as the crowds part, and I can see Jesus. He's standing right in front of the man who'd been calling out to him.

It's now that I realise this man is blind; he's a beggar. He's someone who sits at the gates of the city, begging passersby for money. He's sitting on the dusty ground, lifting his arms up towards Jesus.

"Call him," Jesus said quietly.

At once, those near the man said to him, "Cheer up, get up, he's calling you."

And the blind man jumped up and came closer to Jesus.

Quietly, Jesus asks, "What do you want from me?"

"Teacher, I want to see!" comes the reply.

"Then see!" says Jesus.

At once, the man can see. He has a big smile on his face, and he's shouting out something different now. "I can see!"

The man is looking wildly around him, taking in the crowds, the city, and the smiling face of Jesus. The look of wonder and surprise on his face is something I'll never forget.

I blink and rub my eyes. My brain is trying to understand what's just happened right in front of my eyes. The blind beggar can see again.

Those around us from Jericho who know this man start shouting out, "God is good!" Everyone is astonished and amazed at what we've just seen.

As for Jesus, he simply disappears into the crowd.

"Amazing, just amazing," says Dad, smiling to himself.

I wonder if Dad's remembering the first time he met Jesus and the amazing thing that happened that day.

We're both too amazed to speak, so we walk on in silence for a while, through the city streets.

It's getting late, so we set about finding some food and a place to sleep for the night.

"Only one more day and we'll be in Jerusalem," says Dad. He still hasn't said anything more about what we saw.

I guess there are some things you just can't put into words.

10

JESUS IN JERUSALEM

I'm so excited. Today I'm going to see the holy city of Jerusalem. My feet are going to walk its holy streets, and I'm going to celebrate my first Passover there.

It's the final part of the journey, but I don't feel tired. I can't wait to get my first glimpse of Jerusalem. Walking behind Jesus, the time passes easily.

Dad tells me how it felt for him the first time he came to the city. I can see he's really excited to be sharing this with me.

I'm so busy listening to him that I almost miss the moment.

Everyone has stopped and is standing still and silent. It's only then that I notice we're standing on the brow of a hill. Across the valley is Jerusalem, the holy city.

It's majestic city walls rise high on the hillside. Jerusalem, the home of our fathers, the Temple of God, the City of David. It's a holy moment.

Out of the corner of my eye, I notice Jesus. He's sending a couple of his disciples away.

Quietly, he tells them, "Go into the village ahead. You'll find a donkey tied up and a colt with her. Untie them and bring them to me."

Everyone waits with Jesus, contented just to be here on the Mount of Olives, looking across at the walls of the city. It's hard to describe, but there's a sense of joy bubbling up within me, within everyone around me, just to be standing here in this special place.

After we wait for a while, Jesus's friends bring a donkey for him to ride on, and we're ready to take the last few steps towards the City.

As we walk down the hillside towards the city, through the olive trees, everyone is praising God. "Hosanna!" people are shouting. "Blessed is He!" People throw branches, even garments, down in Jesus's path, calling out to Him. "Hosanna!"

Everyone is happy, shouting and singing, so thankful to God for sending Jesus to us—Jesus, the one whose touch can heal, make the blind see, who makes the impossible possible.

As we walk towards Jerusalem behind Jesus on his donkey, even my dad is shouting out now, "Hosanna to the son of David!"

The crowds pour out of the city gates towards us. They're waving palm branches, freshly cut from the trees, to lay on the ground before Jesus.

THE BIG CATCH OF FISH

What a welcome! The noise is deafening. Everyone's shouting and smiling, excited that Jesus is here.

As we go through the vast gates to Jerusalem, the city is buzzing, alive. It's thrilling to be here.

I feel like maybe I'm in a dream, that this can't be real. I'm here—I'm actually here in Jerusalem. With Dad. With Jesus.

The noise and smells are amazing. As we walk through the narrow streets, the merchants shout out to encourage us to buy. The smell of food from the roadside stalls wafts under our noses.

As I look up, I can see the high walls of the temple towering above me. Walking through the streets of the city, I try to take it all in. I want to remember this moment forever.

Strolling through the winding streets, we arrive at the inn where we're staying. Everyone there is talking about the amazing events of the day.

I make new friends with Rufus and Alexander. They're brothers; they live not too far from the sea. My dad and their dad, Simon, can talk about fishing for hours.

As we share a meal around the table, we all start to tell stories about Jesus.

Dad tells Simon about the day Jesus touched him. I tell Rufus and Alexander my story about the big catch of fish. Everyone loves how Jesus fed the crowds with just my packed lunch!

As I lie in bed, I can't sleep. My mind is buzzing. I'm so excited, so happy.

JENNIFER CARTER

I can't help but think that something really amazing is about to happen.

11

UNEXPECTED EVENTS

Exploring Jerusalem is amazing. There are new sights at the turn of every corner. We walk around with Simon, Rufus, and Alexander, telling stories, laughing, and making jokes.

Dad's new friend Simon is tall and strong. It's so good to see Dad and him smiling and talking together. Simon is even stronger than my dad. He has muscles on his muscles!

Rising early the next day, we push our way into the temple courtyard, eager to sit and listen to Jesus talking there. We sit and listen to the words he speaks, bringing hope and peace to my heart.

We walk around the city together, enter the temple together, and eat our meals at the inn together. As we eat, we hear people telling stories about Jesus.

We're all surprised to hear that not long after we left, Jesus had overturned the tables of the merchants selling goods in the temple courts.

"It's about time someone stood up for what was right," comments Dad.

Later, I hear him talking quietly with Simon when he thinks I'm not listening. He's asking him if he thinks Jesus could be the one promised by God, the one who will set us free from our Roman rulers.

That's a day we all dream of, the day when we'll finally be free from the Roman invaders who rule over us.

Our days in Jerusalem pass in a whirl. We wait and count the minutes until it's the day we will share the Passover meal together. It's going to be mine and Rufus's first Passover in Jerusalem.

Our wait is almost over. It's the night before the Passover meal, and I lie awake. How can I sleep when I feel so excited? At last I drift off to sleep, dreaming of all that we have seen in the Holy City and of all that has happened while imagining what tomorrow will be like.

We're awoken early the next morning by the sound of loud knocking at our door.

Bang, bang, bang. Someone's in a hurry.

Dad stumbles out of bed and opens the door.

It's Simon. "Come quick! They've taken Jesus!" he says.

"They've what?" asks Dad, now wide awake with surprise.

"They've held a court in the night and condemned him."

No-one speaks. None of us knows what to say.

We can't believe it. It seems like we've woken up in a bad dream. We run from the room, pulling our clothes on and running into the streets.

How can this be happening? Just days ago, everyone was welcoming Jesus into the city.

How has everything changed so quickly? And what will happen now?

12

EVERYTHING CHANGES

Even though it's early morning, we can hear the sounds of the crowd. We run, panting and out of breath, all the way to the Roman camp.

We arrive just in time to see something terrible. In the early light, the soldiers bring a man out before the angry crowd.

Jesus? Can it really be you?

Blood runs down this man's face, dripping down from the spikes of the circle of thorns on his head. This man's body is covered with bruises. The skin on his back is torn and broken. Surely this can't be Jesus?

Yet I'd know His eyes anywhere. It's Jesus all right.

What have they done to him? Why have they done this to him?

Helpless, we stand and watch together, looking on as Jesus is forced to carry a huge wooden cross.

We watch as His legs struggle to carry its weight.

Oh, Jesus, why are they being so cruel to you? I wonder.

The tears fill my eyes, running down my cheeks, tasting salty in my mouth.

As the day dawns, we realise that something awful is happening—something unimaginable.

They lead Jesus out, and we follow as he carries the cross through the narrow city streets.

Just when I think it can't get any worse, the crowd start shouting at him, waving their fists and jeering, "Save yourself!"

Behind Jesus, a handful of women follow. They're sobbing, their eyes swollen and red with tears.

The four of us follow. No-one says a word. We can't believe that this is happening. It feels like I'm in a bad dream.

Dad is silent. He's never silent. That can't be good.

We continue to follow behind Jesus, watching his every move.

Suddenly I'm thinking of all the impossible things that Jesus has done. Can he make right all the bad things that are happening? Could he really be the one sent from God to save the Jews?

Jesus stumbles again under the weight of the cross. His knees crash to the ground. His face contorts in pain as he struggles to rise from the hard ground.

The Roman soldier in charge looks across at the crowds. Everyone looks down at the ground, afraid of catching his eye, afraid of what might happen.

"You!" he says, looking straight at Simon. "Carry the cross for him," he orders.

Simon has no choice. Everyone knows that you must either obey the Roman soldiers or be punished for disobeying.

Turning his head to Dad, Simon whispers, "Keep my boys safe." Head high, without looking back, he steps forward.

Then we watch as Jesus struggles to His feet.

The soldiers place the massive wooden cross on Simon's back. Even Simon staggers under its weight as he carries the cross for Jesus.

Dad turns to us boys, his face pale. "Get back to the inn. Go straight back. Run all the way. Stay there and don't leave, whatever happens," he says. Turning to Rufus and Alexander, he whispers, "I'm going to see if I can help your father," and he strides off into the crowds.

Soon he is out of sight, and we are on our own in this city, which now feels angry and hostile.

We begin to run.

13

AN ENDING

We make our way back to the inn in silence, running as fast as we can but staying together. The city streets that seemed so welcoming now feel cold and unfriendly.

We move quickly until we're safely back at the inn, thankful to be somewhere safe.

Alone in my room, my mind begins to wonder. I'm confused by everything that we've seen. How could all the good things have gone wrong so quickly?

I remember the crowds of people welcoming Jesus into the city only a few days ago, shouting, "Hosanna!"

Today we saw them lead him out and make him carry a cross.

A cross. A brutal killing machine that only someone as cruel as the Romans could dream up.

I know what's happening now. I close my eyes to shut out the thoughts, but then the images only grow stronger.

Leaving my room, I knock at Rufus and Alexander's door, not wanting to wait alone. They open the door silently then nod to me to come in.

None of this seems real. Time passes slowly, but we stay in the room, afraid of what's happening outside in the city. We wait, passing the hours as best we can, not knowing what to do, not knowing what will happen.

We watch as the sky grows dark outside—so dark we can barely see across the room even though it's the middle of the day. Then we hear the thunder roaring over our heads. It's so loud it sounds as if God Himself is roaring over the city.

After what seems like hours, the darkness passes, and light enters the room again.

We keep waiting. Hoping.

At nightfall, Dad and Simon come through the door. We rush up to them, hugging them, so happy to see that they're safe. Dad holds me so tight that it feels as if he's crushing me.

"What happened?" we ask.

"He's gone. Dead. They killed him," whispers Dad.

"You're sure?" I ask, scarcely able to believe what he is saying.

"Yes, we watched and waited for a miracle. For a while, nothing seemed to happen," said Dad. "Then the sky grew dark...so dark. Jesus cried out and then was gone."

THE BIG CATCH OF FISH

"The soldiers pierced his side with a spear to make sure he was really gone. No-one could believe it. Jesus was dead. His lifeless body hanging from the cross was proof enough of that. We stayed a while, watching as some of Jesus's friends took him down from the cross and carried his body away."

For a while, none of us speak. What is there to say?

Dad looks up and breaks the silence. "It's late, boys. Time for bed. I guess we should try and get some sleep."

Lying on the bed, my mind is wide awake.

Jesus is gone. I can't believe my friend is gone—that they killed him.

Images play in my mind, and pictures of Jesus flash through it. I remember each moment with him: the big catch of fish, when he touched Dad, when he healed Jaala, when my packed lunch fed a huge crowd, and when he healed a blind beggar.

All I want is to see Jesus again. To see him smile at me again. To hear him laugh. To be with him, just one more time.

Finally, I drift off to sleep, whispering a prayer: "Please, please, can you make everything okay again?"

I long for all the sad things to become untrue. For Jesus somehow to do the impossible, just one more time.

14

THE JOURNEY HOME

With heavy hearts, we leave Jerusalem the very next morning. We can't wait to leave the city that had first brought us such joy and then such sorrow.

It's a long, tiring journey home. All the excitement that we'd felt on the long walk to the Holy City has gone, snuffed out when we heard what happened to Jesus.

None of it makes sense. How could it have happened?

Each step of the journey home is made with heavy hearts. Each step away from the Holy City I'm thinking about my friend, about Jesus.

And I'm remembering him....

I remember the amazing things I've seen.

I remember Jesus on the donkey as we enter Jerusalem. The crowds shouting "Hosanna!"

I remember walking the streets of the Holy City.

Then I remember the angry crowds and the awful news about Jesus.

I remember something Jesus talked about; I didn't understand it at the time.

He spoke about a man who would be hurt, rejected, and killed. He spoke about a cross.

I remember Peter asking Jesus to tell him what it meant.

Jesus also spoke about a man, saying that after three days this man would rise again. I remember him saying that because it made Peter so angry. Rise again? What does that even mean?

Jesus did so many impossible things.

I watched him do them.

He fed thousands with my little lunch of loaves and fishes.

He healed my father, gave him his life back.

He touched Jaala's lifeless body, and she breathed again.

Jesus turned everything I thought I knew upside down.

Is Jesus's story really over? Or could there be another surprise in store?

His words about rising again give me a small flicker of hope. After all that has happened in Jerusalem, might there be a way after all?

Rise again? Could these words mean what I think they might? Dare I hope again?

Might Jesus be able to do the impossible, just one more time?

With hope in my heart, I keep dreaming that Jesus might surprise me again, just one last time.

15

THE STRANGER ON THE SHORE

Even though it's been just a few days, our trip to Jerusalem seems so long ago.

My heart feels sad. I don't understand what happened to Jesus or why. He said such amazing things, did such amazing things. Then he was gone, and now it seems that his amazing story is over.

To help pass the time, I come down with Dad to clean the nets. Dad goes out in the boat with Peter, hoping to catch fish on the lake during the night. It is so good to see Peter here in Galilee.

We all hope that our love of fishing will take our minds off of everything that's happened. I am too tired to go out fishing, and Dad says I should go home. But I want to stay here by the lake. So I jump into a small boat that's pulled up on the shore and lie there, looking up at the sky.

Lying in the bottom of the boat, I can smell fish and hear the sound of waves lapping on the shore. I can see the stars and lie there picking out the patterns in the dark sky.

The sound of the water and the warmth of the air make me feel sleepy. I let the sound of the water wash over me, allowing sleep to finally come.

Sleeping, tossing, turning... I dream of Jesus. I dream of the big catch of fish, of Jesus touching my dad, of him feeding the crowds, of riding the donkey into Jerusalem.

Then I picture the angry crowds. They take him, and Jesus is gone.

Every night since Jerusalem, Jesus comes to me in my dreams. I think about him during the day. When I sleep, he's there.

When I wake, I feel warm rays of sun on my arms. I can hear voices in the distance. Sounds carry across the lake in the early morning, and it's reassuring to hear Dad and Peter's voices from the boat.

In the quiet of the early morning, I love having the little beach to myself. I love to draw in the sand, creating patterns with my fingers.

Pulling myself up, I peer over the edge of the boat. There's someone on the beach. My beach. He's standing there with a fire of burning coals by his feet. He's cooking fish over the fire.

Mmm, that's a good smell!

Fresh fish for breakfast—that's the best breakfast for any boy whose dad is a fisherman.

THE BIG CATCH OF FISH

The figure is turned away from me, so I can't see his face. Who is he? Why is he here?

The boats come in closer to the shore after their long night spent fishing.

The figure on the shore calls out to the men on the boat, "Have you caught anything?"

Across the lake, I hear Peter call back, shaking his head, "No."

The figure calls out to Peter, "Throw your net in to the right. You'll find some there."

It's like watching slow motion as the men cast the net out to the right, trying one last time for a good catch.

In moments, the water is alive, splashing and shimmering. They're pulling in the nets filled to overflowing with fish.

It's another amazing catch, just like the day of the big catch with Jesus.

Wait a minute!

There's something that feels familiar about this figure. There's something familiar about what's happening too.

It's just like the first day I met Jesus, the day we had the big catch of fish.

If only he'd turn around so I could see his face!

Is it a dream? Or could it possibly be true? For the first time in days, a smile creeps across my face.

"It's Jesus," shouts Peter, jumping out of the boat and right into the water. Peter's strong arms help him stride and swim quickly to the shore.

Following him, the fishermen bring the boats in close to shore, dragging the net full of fish behind them.

Jesus...can it really be Jesus?

I can hardly believe what's happening right in front of me.

"Come, let's have some breakfast," says the figure, turning and hugging Peter.

The other fishermen jump out of the boat and greeted this stranger on the beach.

Jesus? Can it really be you? I have to find out for myself.

At once, I'm out of the boat and running. Can it really be him?

16

THE BEST SURPRISE EVER

As I run, my eyes are fixed on the figure on the shoreline. At last, the figure turns around, handing a cooked fish to Simon Peter. He's smiling. Now I can see his face.

It's Jesus! Jesus is alive!

Jesus looks at me, smiles, and opens his arms wide. I run as fast as I can, straight into his arms.

"Jesus!"

As he hugs me, I feel so warm and happy.

"Breakfast?" he asks me. He doesn't have to ask twice.

We sit together on the shore, the freshly cooked fish melting in our mouths. The sun warms us as it rises higher in the sky. But none of these things seem to matter. He's alive. Jesus is here!

After all the sad things that happened, I'm sitting here with Jesus.

JENNIFER CARTER

I feel like laughing, smiling, jumping, dancing. I'm so happy that I don't know what to do!

Jesus is alive! I think this must be the best surprise ever!

We sit around the fire, sharing food together, each of us so happy just to be with Jesus, to spend time with him.

The sadness of the past few days is gone. Our faces and hearts are filled with amazement and wonder.

17

HE'S ALIVE!

After sharing food together, I remember how sad everyone has been. I realise that I can't keep this news to myself.

Running, tripping, skipping, I race to tell the news, shouting out to anyone and everyone.

"He's alive!" I shout to the sky.

"He's alive!" I tell the birds and the trees.

"Jesus is alive," I call out to Jaala.

"He's alive!" I shout to the sheep in the fields, as I run past.

That's Jaala's dad on the horizon, "Jesus is alive!" I tell him.

And as I run, I smile. A big beaming smile. As if I know the biggest secret of all and I want to tell the whole world.

All the sad things are untrue after all. Everything's going to be okay.

JENNIFER CARTER

Jesus is alive!

18

A NEW BEGINNING

A New Beginning

So now you know about my friend Jesus.

This is not the end of the story. It's only the beginning.

When Jesus died, it sounded like the end, but that day by the lakeshore was a new beginning. He's alive!

That day I was so excited that I couldn't help telling everyone about what I'd seen. Peter was the same; he wanted to tell people about Jesus and everything that he'd heard him teach and seen him do.

Now thousands of people know this same Jesus that I was on the shore with that day.

If you meet him, I hope that you'll be friends with him too. Tell him I said hello!

19

ONE MORE THING

If you've enjoyed this book, please consider leaving a rating or review.

20

OTHER BOOKS BY THE AUTHOR

If you've enjoyed this book, you might enjoy other Bible stories re-imagined for children.

A Christmas Surprise, tells the story of the very first Christmas and how Jesus arrived in this world as a baby.

Rediscover the Christmas story through four short stories that tell the story of the birth of baby Jesus - as seen by the donkey in the stable, the shepherds on a hillside, the star gazing down on the little town of Bethlehem, and the baby's mother, Mary.

The Boy and the Battle is a re-imagining of the epic battle between the boy David and the giant, Goliath.

When listening to this story, you'll be able to picture the scene, perhaps imagine yourself as David and understand that this is a real story, about a real person, just like you.

www.ingramcontent.com/pod-product-compliance
Lightning Source LLC
Chambersburg PA
CBHW070758050426
42452CB00012B/2398